FENG SHUI
FOR ABUNDANCE

DAVID DANIEL KENNEDY

FENG SHUI
FOR ABUNDANCE

SOUNDS TRUE

Sounds True, Inc. Boulder, CO 80306
© 2005 David Daniel Kennedy

Published 2005
Printed in Korea

ISBN 1-59179-248-7

Library of Congress Control Number: 2004117958

Ten Emperor Coins on cover and interior artwork designed exclusively by the Yun Lin Temple

Audio Learning Programs by David Daniel Kennedy from Sounds True:
Feng Shui Home Study Course

Table of Contents

Foreword

BY HIS HOLINESS GRANDMASTER LIN YUN RINPOCHE

I am very happy to write the foreword for this book. David Kennedy offers an array of important methods to help you increase your abundance. Even though this book is small, its value cannot be measured by its size. Its content is very precious, especially the two meditation methods that help enhance your spiritual ability—the Meditation to Establish the Foundation and the Activation of the Spiritual Power of the Eight Trigrams.

David identifies important areas you can adjust in the home, yard, and workplace. These address accumulating wealth, letting helpful people appear in life when one is in need, developing one's career smoothly and successfully, and enhancing wisdom and virtue.

You will learn special spiritual cures such as the six-color flags, the small Buddha statue, the small ship, and others. David discusses the importance of your office, the optimal position for your office desk, and other ways to increase spiritual ability, commanding ability, health, wisdom, and peace.

He introduces how to apply Feng Shui's power, both mundane and transcendental, to turn undesirable life circumstances and uncomfortable living and working conditions into comfortable, healthy, and happy environments. David goes further and explains where the wealth positions are and how to adjust them so that your environment will bring you more peace, health, and wealth. Other methods, such as the Sixteen Methods to Nourish One's Health, will further bring longevity, health, and good luck.

The spiritual aspect of Feng Shui is that it works when you are sincere. It is important to perform the Three Secrets Reinforcement and use the *Zi* (11:00 p.m. to 1:00 a.m.) or *Wu* (11:00 a.m. to 1:00 p.m.) hours when performing spiritual cures.

David provides you with an array of methods you can use without studying Buddhism or changing your religion. Even if you are not religious, you can benefit from the methods in this book.

Please read this book carefully and practice its methods with sincerity. By so doing, you will receive unexpected benefits. You will also better help your family and friends cultivate positive merit by doing good deeds, assisting others, and giving to the world.

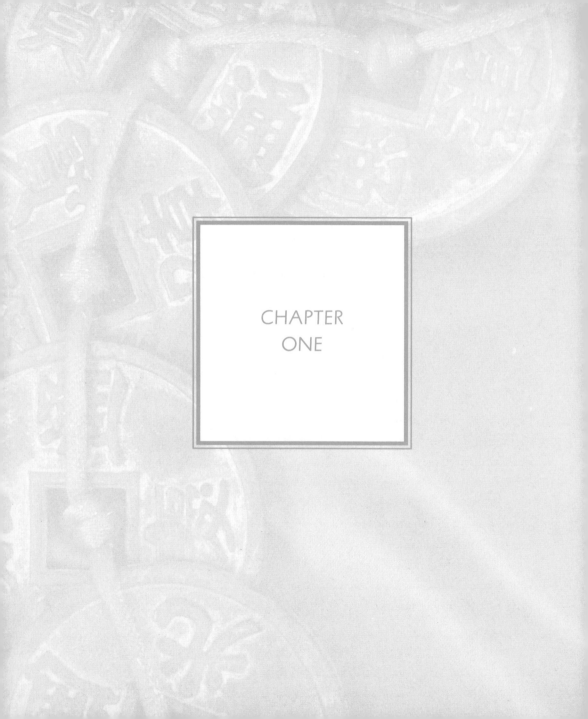

CHAPTER
ONE

Feng Shui and Abundance

FENG SHUI HAS BECOME popular worldwide for a simple reason—it helps people live happier, healthier, and more abundant lives. Feng Shui helps you create positive change in your life by improving the energy flows of your home, property, body, and mind. It does this by deepening your connection with your living environments, and arranging these environments in powerful, harmonious ways.

Your environment profoundly affects every aspect of your life. An out-of-sync or imbalanced home or office space creates undesirable effects that can range from mild discomfort to profound alienation to loss. Feng Shui unlocks the mystery of the relationship between you and your surroundings. In addition, it provides both practical and spiritual methods for cultivating harmony, peace, and beauty that yield inner and outer abundance. You can improve the flow of energy in your home and strengthen inner abundance at the same time. This can help you shape your destiny, enliven your relationships, and reap both tangible and intangible benefits. These are the purposes, the promises, and the fruits of Feng Shui.

Human beings have always craved abundance and prosperity, and have devised innumerable methods and schemes to try to acquire them. No doubt, our more ambitious prehistoric ancestors went that extra mile to acquire and set aside an extra hunk of saber-toothed tiger for a rainy day. Like them, our desire for more (whether meat, caviar, or green stuff: cash-ola) brings up the practical question, "How do I get it?" Today, in our quest for abundance, we don't have to worry about ending up as kitty food. Plus, we have Feng Shui solutions (among other things) that weren't available to cave dwellers. Lucky us!

Abundance is not just about having lots of money and things. Abundance in Feng Shui means a surplus of qi—life force energy—and an inner and outer balance that manifests spiritual and material fruits over and above mere subsistence.

NOTE: You might have seen the term qi spelled "chi" or "ki"; these terms all refer to the same force.

In the deepest sense, abundance is a spiritual quality; we are impoverished or abundant first within our consciousness, and then in the material realm. (As within, so without. As above, so below.) Our spirits know this to be true, but our socialized personalities tend to equate abundance almost exclusively with material wealth.

True abundance results from living in balance and harmony. Creating an atmosphere of peace and calm is priceless, and far better than worrying constantly about money, money, money. Only then, can you make proper decisions and take the actions that bring prosperity your way.

ABOUT THIS BOOK

Feng Shui for Abundance is a book and CD learning tool to help you fulfill the promises of Feng Shui in your life. In this book, I concentrate on Feng Shui methods for achieving these aims. With simple, easy-to-understand concepts and methods, I give practical advice on how to transform both your space and your life. You will learn basic and advanced methods for improving your energy and the energies of your home and office.

The powerful meditation techniques I give you combine with practical methods to bring Feng Shui to life in your daily experience. You will learn how to open the channels within and around you and make positive life changes. The benefits of Feng Shui are the increased abundance, vitality, and health that naturally result from a balanced flow of energy.

Feng Shui for Abundance will also help you achieve:

- An increased awareness of the energy that surrounds and affects you
- An understanding of how this energy flows, or is obstructed, in your home or office
- An increased ability to create conscious, beautiful, harmonious, and vibrant environments

Many people are unaware of the powerful link between meditation and Feng Shui. That link is qi, the vital energy that animates all living things. Both Feng Shui and meditation are forms of qi circulation and cultivation. One is more external, and the other more internal, but both improve the flow and balance of your energy. They are the yin and yang of Feng Shui.

A MULTIFACETED APPROACH

Feng Shui works on the physical plane by arranging and harmonizing objects in physical space. It also works to affect change at a more subtle level by stimulating you toward action or inaction, clarity or confusion. Your body, mind, and spirit are as much a part of your environment as are your external surroundings, such as your home or office. Yet, many people fall into the trap of putting all their Feng

GRANDMASTER LIN YUN RINPOCHE AND FENG SHUI
The style of Feng Shui I present in this book is Black Sect Tantric Buddhist Feng Shui (or BTB Feng Shui). BTB Feng Shui focuses on the qi of the person as well as the environment, helping to bring both to a more uplifted state. As taught by Grandmaster Lin Yun, it integrates spiritual methods and modern teachings with the traditions of Feng Shui practice. When I refer to Feng Shui in this book, I am referring to this multi-faceted approach.

Shui eggs into one basket and focusing solely on one facet, such as furniture placement or color selection. This limited approach can produce positive life effects, but it may not create enough power for optimal results.

Feng Shui is most effective when applied in a multilayered fashion. Improving your life through Feng Shui involves adjusting and developing your inner and outer environments according to the principles of energy flow. We know a chain is only as strong as its weakest link. Feng Shui helps you strengthen key links in your chain of life.

I present abundance within a larger paradigm than the conventional "getting a bunch of stuff I really want" approach. Yes, Feng Shui can help you get a bunch of stuff you really want. But abundance is much deeper and richer than that. And that deeper abundance is what Feng Shui is all about. My hope is to give you real-world solutions to your energetic problems, increasing your abundance through:

Environmental cures: Feng Shui solutions for your home and office
Spiritual methods: Little-known yet highly effective Feng Shui techniques
Personal qi exercises: Cultivating your body, mind, and spirit
Meditation methods: The highest level of Feng Shui practice

This is an ample menu to choose from as your circumstances and needs require. These useful methods support each other to create true changes in your life.

QI: LIFE FORCE ENERGY

Qi is the cornerstone of Feng Shui. It is the life force that animates your body and circulates in your environment, for good or ill. Feng Shui improves your environment's energy flow, creating a positive impact on your personal energy.

Grandmaster Lin Yun says, "Feng Shui relates to the individual's qi. Qi is the true essence of our life, and the vitality of our life. Qi moves our brain so we can think, moves our tongue so we can speak, moves our legs so we can walk, and moves our hand so we can write."

MAPPING YOUR SPACE FOR ABUNDANCE

In Feng Shui, you use special techniques to determine the areas of your environment that correspond with aspects of your life. This way you know where to start making necessary changes.

One of these methods applies the *Ba-Gua* concept. The Ba-Gua maps the locations of nine life aspects in your space. These are:

- Family
- Wealth or Money
- Fame and Reputation
- Marriage
- Children
- Benefactors and Travel
- Career
- Self-Cultivation
- Health

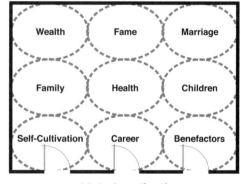

1.1 Ba-Gua on Floor Plan

Illustration 1.1 depicts their arrangement in your space.

You can place this mapping tool over your home floor plan, your lot plan, your bedroom, or your office. Because we are focusing on abundance, we will emphasize three of the nine areas: Wealth, Career, and Health, located in the back left, front center and center areas of the space, respectively.

Note that the front entrance to a space can be located in one of only three areas of the Ba-Gua: Benefactors, Career, or Self-Cultivation. These are the only options for the main entrance; it cannot be in the Family, Wealth, Fame, Marriage, or Children areas. When we discuss Wealth areas in this book, please see this section for reference.

AN EXCITING JOURNEY

Fasten your seat belt for an exciting exploration of Feng Shui methods to increase your abundance. First, we will address Wealth areas of your home, then the abundance-generating power of your workspace. We will also reveal spiritual methods, health cultivation techniques, and meditations.

I hope you enjoy working with *Feng Shui for Abundance* as much as I enjoyed creating it. May your Feng Shui adventure bear rich fruits of abundance, harmony, and peace.

CHAPTER
TWO

Activating Your Wealth Areas

FENG SHUI OFFERS you multiple methods for creating and maintaining abundance by optimizing the energy flow in key areas of your home. You will discover why particular areas are important, and how to increase your flow of abundance with simple Feng Shui cures. You'll find out how to:

- Find the key Wealth areas of your home environment
- Activate your main entrance
- Use Feng Shui cures to improve the energy in your Wealth areas
- Use flowing water for abundance

Be sure to use the Three Secrets Reinforcement as an integral part of all the cures in this book. See Chapter 8 for details.

FINDING KEY WEALTH AREAS
The Ba-Gua maps the Wealth area of your home (house or apartment) as the *back left corner* or area of the space. (The front of the home is the area containing the front door.)

Additional Wealth areas, including the back left portions of your master bedroom, property and office, are also cornerstones of abundance (see Illustration 2.1). Once you've identified these areas, you can assess the energies there and perform Feng Shui cures. Performing cures in multiple Wealth areas is definitely more effective than attending to just one.

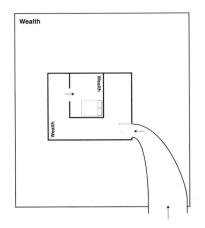

2.1 Wealth areas of Lot, House, and Bedroom

USING CURES

There are many solutions for stimulating and increasing your abundance. In Feng Shui, we refer to these methods as "cures." Once you have identified the Wealth areas of your environment, here are some cures you can use to enhance the qi flow:

- Crystal spheres
- Mobiles
- Wind chimes
- Plants

These cures work in multiple ways to increase and harmonize the energy flows in your space.

Crystal spheres expand and brighten the energy (see Illustration 2.2); chimes attract abundance qi and enhance clarity. Mobiles stimulate and balance the energy flow in the area, while plants add growth, vitality, and new life energy. All of these can be effective solutions depending on your needs and preferences. Use them according to the methods I outline in the pages ahead.

Hang crystal spheres, wind chimes, and mobiles using a red ribbon that you have cut to a multiple of nine inches in length. The red ribbon is an important part of your cure, providing additional strength and effectiveness. See the Appendix on page 95 for additional cure details.

Another helpful method is to use purple in the Wealth area. Because purple corresponds to wealth, the more you use, the more effective your cure. Decorate this area with purple accents, such as curtains, pillows, a bedspread, or artwork with a purple

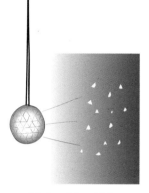

2.2 Faceted Crystal Sphere

theme. Alternatively, paint one or two walls, the ceiling, or the entire room purple. (Though cheaper than a paint job, wearing purple-tinted glasses is probably not a "do-it-yourself" abundance cure.)

FINDING MISSING AREAS

When diagnosing the Wealth area of your home, first determine if any of it is "missing" from your home's layout, as this can cause financial difficulties. Missing areas occur where there is a gap of less than half of the length of the wall or side you are considering. (If you live in a medieval castle, your dungeon *is not* a Wealth area, unless you turn it into a wine cellar or an in-law unit.) Also, check your master bedroom, office, and lot to see if there are missing areas in their back left sections. (see Illustration 2.3.)

On the other hand, if you have a projecting or extra area in the back left portion of your residence, yard or bedroom, you can experience additional monetary benefit (see Illustration 2.4).

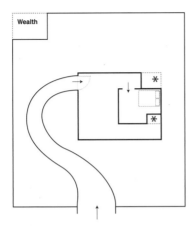

2.3 Missing Wealth areas of Lot,
House and Bedroom

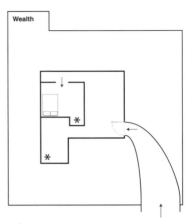

2.4 Projecting Wealth areas of Lot,
House and Bedroom

CURING MISSING AREAS

For a missing portion in the Wealth area of
either an apartment or master bedroom, a good solution is to put mirrors on both the

walls that border the missing space. For best results, these mirrors should cover all or most of the walls in question. If some of the Wealth area of the lot is missing, you can place purple flowering plants to enliven the area.

An excellent cure for a missing portion in the Wealth area of your home is to place a large fountain outside the house at the location of the missing corner (see Illustration

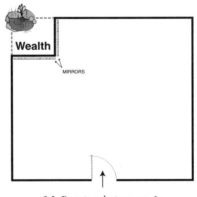

2.5 Fountain and mirror cures for
missing Wealth area

2.5). If you have a healthy tree in this area, voilà, you already have a cure in place. Simply do the Three Secrets Reinforcement, to add spiritual energy (see Chapter 8). You can further strengthen your wealth by hanging a quality wind chime on a red ribbon from the tree.

PROTECTING YOUR ABUNDANCE

Be on the lookout for drains in your Wealth area, as drains there can be a source of financial loss. Bathroom drains, especially toilets, or exit doors in the Wealth area can be particularly troubling.

A bathroom in the back left of your dwelling can drain resources. An effective cure is to mount a full-length mirror on the outside of the bathroom door. Use a large high-quality mirror rather than the discount closet-door variety. Keep this door closed consistently, as the mirror cure is ineffective if the bathroom door stands open. You can also apply these cures to a bathroom located in the back left or Wealth area of the master bedroom.

Sometimes a back door or patio door opens directly out of the Wealth area. I recommend that you hang the special Feng Shui bamboo flute over the door (see Appendix). Hang it at a 45-degree angle, with the right side higher and the left side lower (see Illustration 2.6). To be effective, the flute's ridges should be intact rather than sanded smooth (see Illustration 2.7). Don't let anyone play with or blow the flute, as this can reduce its power.

Another solution is to mount a large mirror directly opposite from and reflecting the exit door. This energetically

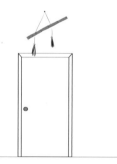

2.6 Special Bamboo Flute over door

2.7 Special Bamboo Flute detail

"moves" the door from its unfortunate position in the Wealth area. You can use this door as before.

RELEASING STUCK QI

Clutter and unused items in the Wealth area of your home can create stuck or stagnant energy. Free this energy by organizing or clearing them out. Today, buckaroo! Piles of debris in the back left of the yard can also block your abundance. If you dump them in another living area, you will simply create obstacles in another part of your life. (Feng Shui is *not* the art of rearranging chaos.) Also, pay attention to the back left area of your bedroom and office, particularly if you have closets there. Use common sense in assessing the area. If something needs to be there, fine; just make sure it's clean and organized.

An outbuilding in the Wealth area of your property, such as a shed or garage, can lead to increased wealth as it adds "weight" to that part of the property. However, this can also indicate that one partner has hidden financial resources, or it may contribute to such a situation. (If they are *your* hidden finances, you might want to resolve the underlying issues, as unhealthy secrets in a relationship represent an internal Feng Shui drain.) To prevent this, put a sizable convex mirror on the house wall that is closest to and facing the other building. Use the Three Secrets Reinforcement, visualizing that the partners' finances are linked together.

On the other hand, a structure that is open and that you can see through is very beneficial for the Wealth area of your property. For example, a gazebo in the Wealth area of the yard promotes increased abundance, without the potential drawbacks of

a shed or garage. An octagonal gazebo is especially effective (see Illustration 2.8).

NURTURING THE CENTER

You can powerfully nurture your abundance
by paying attention to the center areas of your
spaces. The center is important because it is
connects and unifies all the parts. The center
controls and provides energy to the perimeter
areas, which in turn feed energy back to it.
This has practical implications. In a battle, if
a flank is crumbling but the center still holds,

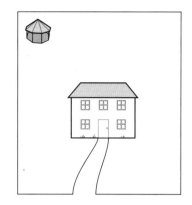

2.8 Gazebo in Wealth area of Lot

there is a chance that the army will survive. But if the center gives way, the army is
scattered and the battle will be lost. So, protect the center at all costs.

In personal qi cultivation, you focus on the center of the body, or the *dan tien*, located
three finger widths below your navel. This is your body's main energy center. The energy
you harvest from qigong, or energy cultivation exercises is stored here. An abundance of
qi in your dan tien gives you vitality, health, and joy. If you deplete this energy, you can
weaken your body, and impair your health and vitality.

The same is true for your dwelling and office. The center is "central" in Feng
Shui. It is where all the energies in the space mingle and interact. The center of your
space is vital not only for your wealth, but also for health, relationships, and other
areas of life. (The Ba-Gua designates this area as Health, but it also refers to the
unity of all areas of life.)

The center affects all areas of your life, so cures at the center can be very powerful. They can strengthen your core energy, and open the flow of solutions that were
previously blocked. You can use center cures when you have a nagging problem you

can't solve, when several areas of your life need help simultaneously, or when you are feeling at your wits' end and don't know which way to turn.

CURING THE CENTER

When assessing the center area, first check for any significant negative placements, which can harm your abundance. The most detrimental are a bathroom or kitchen in the center.

A bathroom located in the center may cause household finances to go "down the tubes." At minimum, a bathroom in the center can use the same cures as given above for a bathroom in the Wealth area. Another solution is not to use this bathroom, especially the toilet, if practical. If you must use a central bathroom regularly, the cure is to fully mirror all of the room's interior walls. (Sitting on the toilet was never so glorious.) If one wall is a tub or shower, you can install a mirrored shower door as one of the mirrored walls. An upstairs bathroom in either the center of the upper floor, or over the center of the main floor, can also benefit from this cure.

A stove in the center of the home can lead to money and health problems, as well as fires or accidents. Hang a crystal sphere or a metal wind chime over the stove, and use the Three Secrets Reinforcement while visualizing peace, safety, and increased abundance.

If the center of your home or office has no obvious Feng Shui bloopers, you can still do beneficial cures in this area. Place fresh green plants to add new life; use nine healthy green plants in the center as a potent solution. (Avoid banyan trees and giant redwoods, as the hole needed in the ceiling is not cost effective, and might be another drain!) Another good cure is to hang a wind chime or crystal sphere in the center using the red-ribbon method described earlier.

ACTIVATING THE MAIN ENTRANCE

Feng Shui masters view the home as similar to the human body. For example, the front door is the "mouth" of the home. The front entrance is a crucial portal through which vital energy enters the dwelling. The more positive and abundant the qi residing at your front entrance, the better your home's overall energy.

The home needs to breathe just as your body does, drawing in positive energy and expelling used, stale, or toxic energy. A positive inflow through the mouth of your home enhances your income and the human relations within the home. Blockages at the front door will create blocks in your income and money flow, and keep new opportunities from reaching you.

Look at your front entryway and the space around your door, both inside and outside. Make sure the door can swing freely and opens all the way to let in sufficient energy. Remove unnecessary items from the pathway, inside and out. In addition, see that nothing is stored behind the door.

Keep your entrance well lit; a dark entrance suppresses the inflow of energy, thereby diminishing your abundance. If you have a dim light, replace it with a brighter one. A broken light fixture or a dead bulb inside or outside the front entrance is like a metaphorical perched vulture, symbolizing "decay" at the entrance, so fix it immediately.

Use a resonant metal wind chime to energize your entry and attract greater abundance. For a house, hang the chime outside the front door; for an apartment, hang it just inside the front door. Your chime should have an appealing ring that continues to resonate after you strike the chime. When you apply this cure, visualize the sound attracting wealth to your home like bees to honey, increasing your abundance. (A giant gong is not recommended unless you live in a castle. And neighborhood children will find them irresistible.)

DRAWING ON THE POWER OF FIRE AND WATER

The primal Feng Shui energies of fire and water are potent forces for promoting and increasing your abundance when you use them appropriately. Properly used, they can help you create balance and harmony in your environment. Fire is yang heat and energy; water is cool yin, liquid flow. We need both for power and harmony (think har-money); both are relevant for income and abundance. Stoves and fountains are two classic forms that fire and water take in the home. Below are two ways to incorporate them to increase your abundance:

- Place flowing water near the entrance, or in a Wealth area.
- Protect the stove, your home's primary energy generator.

Flowing Water for Abundance

A potent cure for increasing abundance is to place flowing water, ideally a quality fountain, near the entrance. (Contrary to Feng Shui urban legend, leaving a running hose on your front porch is not an effective "flowing water cure.") A fountain near the front entrance can stimulate the flow of money, as well as increased social connections and new opportunities. The bigger the water flow, in balance with the surroundings, the more effective the cure. (Where fountains are concerned, size does matter!) A powerful flow of water brings dynamic abundance. However, a small indoor fountain is also effective.

If you live in a house, you can place your fountain outside, near the front door. If you live in an apartment, or lack sufficient space outside your front door, placing a fountain inside the front door is beneficial. A fountain in which water flows down in multiple levels or tiers is a more powerful cure.

Getting Fired Up

The position of your kitchen stove and its working condition can powerfully influence your abundance. Food emerges from the intermingling of human and earthly energies. The cook preparing the food is the human part of the process, and the fire at the stove is the primal earthly part. The disposition of the cook is important; Asian cultures believe that a cook's state of mind while preparing food affects the abundance of the household as well as the digestion. (Genghis Khan always wondered why no one would eat his quiche.)

First, check the stove's position relative to your kitchen entrances. It's important to avoid having your back to a doorway while cooking at the stove. Ideally, all kitchen entries will be visible to the cook when he or she stands at the stove. If you cannot easily see a doorway while looking at the burners (peripheral vision doesn't count), consider it "at your back," even if it's not directly behind you. This principle holds true even if you feel safe while cooking, or live alone and know that no one can approach you from behind when you're at the stove.

In most Western kitchens, the cook will have his or her back to at least one doorway while facing the stove. The cure is to move the door so it is "in front of you" at the stove. Sound impossible? Not with Feng Shui. Place a quality mirror either directly against the wall behind the stove, or on the wall at either side, so that you can conveniently see the door or entry while facing the stove. This visually places the door in front of you as you cook, putting you in the secure position, which leads to greater fortune. (A classic "smoke and mirrors" cure!) You may need mirrors directly behind, to the left, and to the right of the stove to visually catch all the openings to the kitchen.

If the kitchen is part of a great room or large open area (i.e., not a separate room), these mirrors are even more useful. In addition, hang a crystal sphere using a red ribbon over the cook's position at the stove. An optional method is to place a sizable convex mirror directly behind or to one side of the stove that reflects all the kitchen entries.

A stove visible from the front door of the home leaves the cook with virtually no protective barrier against the outside world. This can be a threat to abundance and lead to accidents, setbacks, and loss of money. An ideal solution is to erect a visual block, like a screen or curtain—cloth, wood, or bamboo are good—that hides the stove from immediate view. (Think of it as your own personal Great Wall.)

Alternately, you can hang a crystal sphere or wind chime from the ceiling on a red ribbon between the door and the stove, or over the cook's position in front of the stove. You can apply more than one of these cures, depending on the need.

The position of the stove within the home is also important. In addition to curing a stove in the center, be aware that a stove is generally better in the back of the home than in the front, creating greater safety and household peace. Placing the stove in the Family area of the home's floor plan is fine, while a stove in the Children's area can lead to various problems with children (see Illustration I.I). Place healthy green plants near a stove in the latter position.

Ensuring Optimal Stove Condition

Make sure your stove is in good working condition; it's a prime source of energy for the household. The burners are the most important element. A burner that doesn't work, works inconsistently, or is hard to light can mean impaired wealth-generating power. The cure is quite logical: Fix the burners. (If it's a gas stove, it may also represent a very real danger, so get it checked. Your gas company likely provides free inspections of all gas appliances.) Anything broken or out of order can be a problem. Also, pay close attention to knobs and switches.

Many people fall into the habit of using only one or two of their burners most of the time. The problem is that having unused burners means less abundance-generating energy for the household. For best results, use all your burners over time, as you cook.

Lighting the Kitchen

Your kitchen, a key location for generating energy in the home, should have bright lighting. An insufficiently lit kitchen dims your awareness as you cook, which affects the food you eat. This can translate into less energy, affecting your vitality, health, and abundance. The lights, however, should not be glaring or overly bright.

CHAPTER
THREE

Creating Career Success

JUST AS YOU APPLY Feng Shui energy principles to your home and reap the personal and spiritual benefits of a balanced environment, you can also apply them to your office and thereby profit in your career and finances. Whether you run a home business or go to a workplace daily, the proper use of Feng Shui in a work environment can nourish your spirit, improve your energy and concentration, and even smooth your career path and increase your prosperity. Read on to discover how to augment your career Feng Shui.

PROSPERING IN YOUR HOME OFFICE

A key success factor if you work at home is having a dedicated office or work-space; this holds and conducts power and gives you greater control in your career. A properly Feng Shui'd work environment gives you energy and support from your surroundings. Such an environment won't do all the work for you (dang!), but it will help you unleash and develop your natural talents and skills, prevent needless confusion and frustration, and clear your path to progress and achievement.

Think of your office as Command Central, the seat of authority in your career. Your job is to use Feng Shui to claim and enhance your authority in your career domain. (If you don't, it ain't gonna happen!) How would you design your office space if you viewed yourself as a starship captain in your own *Star Trek* series? How would you arrange your desk, its position, the objects on it, and the furniture surrounding it so that it focused all of your power toward your chosen career destination? Your job is to be the captain, boldly steering your career starship toward your dreams!

This level of Feng Shui is both mystical and very practical. A shift in perspective and in your self-perception (from schlepper to Captain) is more powerful when you combine it with a shift in your physical environment. For example, don't leave your work area in chaos. Don't put your office in a room that you use regularly for other purposes. Imagine yourself sitting at your desk dealing with Klingons intent on sabotaging your career path while in the background, in the heat of battle, we see a half-varnished cabinet covered with old rags, tools scattered about, empty soda cans, and a washing machine rattling noisily in the corner on a spin cycle.

You get the picture. Chaos and cross purposes in your work environment diminish your clarity, your focus, and your authority, and reduce your chances of success. The Klingons will most likely win in the end.

DEDICATING YOUR SPACE

There are many Feng Shui drawbacks to trying to work in a non-dedicated space, such as on a dining room table. Some are obvious, others are subtle. First, you constantly have to set up and take down your work. This wastes time and generates impatience, frustration, and confusion, while stimulating unconscious resistance to work. It also subtly undermines your self-esteem and self-respect. You are on some level telling yourself that you're not *really* serious about success, and that you don't *really* deserve a first-class working environment. Both of these factors are energy leaks that rob you and your career of vitality, clarity, and creativity. Such leaks diminish your capacity to make the best decisions and take the most decisive and beneficial actions.

The above "leak factors" make it harder for you to surmount obstacles, persist in the face of challenges and setbacks, and reach your goals. Having a fixed location that is formally, exclusively, and even ceremonially dedicated to your career establishes a solid inner and outer foundation for success. I have advised many home businesses and I have rarely seen one succeed without a properly dedicated workspace.

If you really can't spare an entire room for your office, then dedicate at least part of a room solely to work. You want your work area to be set apart, giving you sufficient privacy and a sense of control. Create a physical and visual boundary using a curtain, a shoji screen, or even a row of tall plants. You can use a guest bedroom as your office, as long as guests only visit occasionally.

Now that we've covered basic factors of home office Feng Shui, let's move on to issues that apply to either a home office or an outside office. These are desk, desk position, chair, Feng Shui cures, and other vital aspects of success.

POSITIONING YOURSELF FOR ABUNDANCE

Let's discuss the primary matter of proper desk setup. Your desk and its position are as important in your home office as they are in a company workplace. And at home, you get to choose! It is important to choose a real "business style" desk that gives you a sense of power and authority. Your desk is the primary "power object" in your office. So choose a desk that you love, that looks good, and that feels great to sit behind as you survey your kingdom. Equally important is placing it in a good position in the room or workspace that you have dedicated to be your office. Ideally, the room should have a real door that closes, and even locks.

The fundamental principle of power desk placement is called "commanding position." A weak desk position makes your path more difficult than necessary by creating hidden obstacles. A powerful commanding position harmonizes and focuses the energy in your space. It utilizes your sensory awareness and your physical relationship to your environment in a way that enhances your sense of protection and safety, your personal power, and your career abundance.

Commanding position energetically puts you in command of your environment and the situations that occur within it. It also enhances your leadership and authority. If you work with others, it makes you less likely to be interfered with or sabotaged by attacks and backbiting.

But a commanding position should not be overdone, like those trucks you see driving around on five-foot-tall tires, requiring a ladder for riders to climb into the cab. Benito Mussolini was famous for his exaggerated use of the commanding position method. He had his desk placed with his back to the wall at the far end of an enormous marble hall. When someone was ushered into his office, they had to cross nearly a hundred feet of highly polished marble to his desk. This is commanding-position overkill; real power requires a balanced perspective. The methods I give here are about being in command of your life, not obsessively trying to dominate others.

CONTROLLING YOUR TERRITORY

To employ commanding position, first place your chair as far from the door as you practically can. The more space between you and the door, the more territory you command. (But *don't* use a vast marble hall as your office!) You also have maximum time to notice what's happening at the entrance, see who is approaching, and react appropriately.

This principle accommodates our evolutionarily programmed need to be aware of our environment, and to be ready and able to respond to both danger and opportunity.

And it works whether or not you're consciously aware of it, or even believe in it. From an energy perspective, locating yourself farthest from the door puts you in a position to gather maximum qi, and gives you an enhanced strategic position. This usually means that you will be sitting in the opposite corner from the door. If the door is in the center of the wall, you can choose either corner.

Seeing the Door

Next, you want to be able to see the door clearly from your sitting position. This is critically important, as you inherently want to know who or what is approaching you. This is survival instinct, and you are subject to it whether you know it or not. Place your desk so that you see the door in your forward field of vision, and don't have a door or an entryway behind you or at your side. If your office has multiple doors, endeavor to sit where you can see the main door; you can also use the mirror tip below to put any other doors within view.

See a Wider View

The above position should be integrated with the companion principle of seeing the widest scope of the room possible. Sit facing the main expanse of the room, not with your back to the door. This helps for two reasons. It bolsters the subconscious feelings of security and control mentioned above. Also, seeing a wider vista expands your perspective, inspires greater optimism, and supports a future-oriented vision.

Sit Outside the Door Line

You will automatically observe the next maxim if you have followed the first three, but it's important enough to emphasize on its own: The desk should be outside the direct line of the door. If you sit directly in the path of the door, you become vulnerable, and therefore not in command. If this isn't feasible, the cure is to hang a faceted crystal sphere halfway between the door and the desk.

Enjoy Good Backing

An additional point of emphasis for desk positioning is to sit with your back to a solid wall. This is the same principle as positioning a fort in front of a mountain for protection. The mountain provides solid backing and a sense of support, as attackers are less likely to come over a mountain. In the same way, no one can attack you from behind when your back is to the wall. (If they *can* walk through walls, you don't have a chance anyway, so don't worry about it.)

Conversely, sitting with your back to a window or door creates unnecessary vulnerability and distracts your awareness, subtly drawing your attention backward. If you must sit in this position, apply this cure: hang a crystal sphere or wind chime between yourself and the door or window behind you.

Additional Tips

When you place the front of your desk directly against a wall, as is the case in many home desk setups, you lose the view in front of you, you feel blocked (because you are), and you diminish your future-oriented vision. Some feel that having their desk against a window affords them the view and corresponding freedom of thought and creativity. It's a nice theory but one that doesn't seem to hold up in practice. If you have this feeling, I suggest you employ a commanding position that additionally provides a pleasing outer view from a side window or one opposite your desk position.

In a corporate cubicle, you have little choice as to your desk position, and you must depend on Feng Shui cures to bridge the gap. Due to design limitations, you may have little choice as to your setup at home. In either case, if your back is to the door or entrance, there is an effective cure. Place the largest mirror possible in a position that enables you to see the entryway to your space from your typical sitting position. If you need to cover multiple angles or entries to your space, use a large convex mirror. Use the Three Secrets Reinforcement (see Chapter 8) with this cure, as with all your cures.

Effective mirror placement puts your door visually in front of you, which is the preferred position. While this cure is not as good as physically facing the door, it is a good solution yielding true benefits.

Another element to take into account in power desk positioning is the angle at which you place your desk. Since the commanding position is usually near a corner, you can place your desk so that your back is to whichever of the walls feels best (see Illustration 3.1). If you have windows on more than one wall, and proper placement in relation to the door requires that you have your back to a window, choose the smallest window; if the windows are the same size, place your back to the window that opens onto the quietest, least trafficked area.

To help your career take off like a 747, place your desk at an angle, with the corner behind you (see Illustration 3.1). Use this only if it is practical in the space you have, considering all factors. To enhance this angled desk position you can put a plant in the corner behind your chair. You can also place a standing lamp behind the chair that arches up and over the desk.

Having a powerful desk position in a settled location is important, as it imparts a sense of stability and belonging. You don't want to feel like a refugee in your own office.

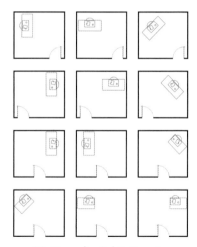

3.1 Commanding Desk Position options

I know of several business firms that failed after trying the "hoteling" workspace concept in which employees used a different workspace every day. A free-floating workspace doesn't make you feel free. Instead, it makes it hard to immerse yourself in your work and generate both creative and productive momentum.

YOUR POWER DESK

Remember, your desk is both your launching pad and the command position in your starship to success. Its quality and characteristics are significant. For the best career achievement, a real desk (ideally an executive-style desk) is virtually always preferable to a table, a table-like desk, a computer desk, or a workstation. (As for a "desk" made from a spare door on two filing cabinets ... well, don't even get me started.) If you're a creative type or an artist who wants to design a uniquely personal desk, just make sure your design doesn't violate good Feng Shui principles. The metaphor of a ship is useful here. You may want your ship to reflect who you are as a person, but you also want it to stay afloat.

An ideal desk features full front and side panels. The length of these panels is important, with longer being better. In particular, a front or modesty panel that extends down to the floor is important for protection at work. A partial, or even worse, missing front panel can result in unwarranted career attacks and vulnerabilities. These principles hold true even when you work by yourself in your home office.

A SOLID SEAT FOR SUCCESS

A good chair is a key foundation for your ongoing success as well as the physical support for the majority of your work life. The Feng Shui of your chair starts with getting a high-quality office chair, not a spare household chair, which can never support your full success. Even if you only sit at work for short periods, your choice of a chair is significant in terms of both Feng Shui and ergonomics.

Physical Support

Ergonomics involves the fit and function of the chair as it relates to your body's need for comfort, support, and movement. There are many specially built ergonomic chairs, and even stores that will custom design a chair to fit you. In the final analysis, you will make your best selection by going to several stores and sitting in a variety of chairs to find the one that fits your body best.

If possible, get a chair that has a height adjustment and doesn't inhibit movement or maneuverability. Chairs that are confining or difficult to maneuver create subtle blocks to your practical functioning and your career progress.

Energetic Support

A good chair, as a personal support and foundation, must provide physical, psychological, and energetic stability and protection against "attacks" or problems. The construction of your chair itself should feature three Feng Shui characteristics:

- A solid chair back is preferred.
- There is no gap between the back and the bottom of the chair.
- A higher chair back is better than a lower one.

Ideally, the back of your chair should be solid, at least the height of your shoulders (higher is better), and with no gap at the base between your lower back and the seat. It should literally "cover your back." This provides a sense of security and full support, enabling you to do your work in the best frame of mind.

FLOWING WATER PLACEMENT

Flowing water is an important Feng Shui tool for increasing cash flow. A fountain placed at the entrance to your office is ideal. You can also put a fountain in the

Wealth spot (back left area) of your office or cubicle, or a small fountain on the back left corner of your desk. (The front of the desk is where your stomach meets the desk.) Reinforce the above cures with the Three Secrets Reinforcement, visualizing your increasing abundance in great detail.

THE CAREER AREA OF YOUR HOME

In addition to improving your office, you can further boost your career by enhancing the Career area in your home. To find it, simply identify the middle third of the front wall of your home, the area of your home that corresponds to your career (see Illustration I.1). The front wall is always the one containing the front door. Cures that you can apply to this area include a fountain, a wind chime, or a crystal sphere hung by a red cord.

IF YOU DON'T HAVE A DESK

You may be a worker who has no set desk, office, or fixed work place. If you are a delivery person, factory worker, masseuse, food server, traveling salesperson, or other mobile employee, how can Feng Shui help you? I recommend that you focus on:

- The Career area of your home (as explained above)
- The Wealth area of your house (see Chapter 2)
- Personal energy cultivation (see Chapters 5 to 7)

EMPOWER THE WEALTH AREA OF YOUR OFFICE

The Wealth area of your personal workspace is important for your career income. This area is easy to find. Standing in the entrance to your office, cubicle, or workspace, point to the farthest back left portion of the space. This is your Wealth area. Now that you've identified this area, you can enhance its energy using the following Feng Shui cures.

First, clear the area of clutter and junk. This opens up the energy flow in your Wealth area. Think of cleaning your Wealth area as panning for gold. You have to wash away the dirt, gravel, and clutter before you can find the hidden treasure.

With the space cleaned and cleared, you can use Feng Shui cures to create new energy that dynamically supports abundance. Place something purple in your wealth area; the more purple you use, the more effective the cure. A fountain is another good choice, since flowing water invites prosperity. You might place purple amethyst in a fountain and combine these two powerful cures.

By following the Feng Shui guidelines offered here, you will create powerful energetic support for your career success.

CHAPTER
FOUR

Special Abundance Methods

CHAPTERS 2 AND 3 cover basic aspects of abundance Feng Shui for your home and office. In this chapter, I reveal some of the hidden spiritual methods for creating abundance, as taught by Grandmaster Lin Yun Rinpoche. These secret methods can enhance your material well-being and your spiritual life as well—a powerful combination. Although these cures are rarely taught and may seem a little foreign to Western thinking, they are uniquely effective for creating positive results.

THE SIX TRUE COLOR LIGHT FLAGS

A powerful, yet rarely disclosed Feng Shui method is the Six True Color Light Flags cure, which draws its power from the potent Buddhist mantra: *Om Mani Padme Hum.* Most religions regard sacred sounds as having great power for healing, transformation, and spiritual growth. This mantra is called the Six True Words, or the Mantra of Compassion. Each of the six syllables helps clear a negative emotion and promotes a benefit.

Syllable	Releases	Promotes
Om	Pride	Generosity
Ma	Jealousy	Righteousness
Ni	Desire	Patience
Pad	Ignorance	Diligence
Me	Greed	Concentration
Hum	Anger	Wisdom

You can receive these benefits by reciting the mantra aloud or silently, or by strategically placing six colored flags representing the mantra in your environment.

Each of the mantra's six syllables corresponds to a specific color. We call these the Six True Colors:

Syllable	Color
Om	White
Ma	Red
Ni	Yellow
Pad	Green
Me	Blue
Hum	Black

You can use this unique cure to create balance and harmony in several ways:

- To increase the flow of abundance in your life
- To solve numerous Feng Shui problems in your environment
- To dispel or heal various chronic or temporary life problems
- To increase energy flow in any area of your home

Constructing the Cure

First, create six flags, one for each of the six syllables or colors. You can easily find cloth in your local fabric shop, or you can make the flags from colored paper or plastic. Make each flag one solid color—white, red, yellow, green, blue, and black. Your flags can be any size you choose, from small (a few inches high), to medium (a foot or two high), to large (several feet high). However, for this cure, the six flags should all be the same size. Your flagpoles should be made from bamboo if possible. Your local garden supply store probably carries thin bamboo poles.

The next step is to write the correct syllable on each of the colored flags. You can use the English, Chinese, or Tibetan mantra syllables (see table below). You only need to use one language. This step is optional; the flags are effective without the syllables.

Flag Color	English Syllable	Chinese Syllable	Tibetan Syllable
White	Om	嗡	ཨོཾ
Red	Ma	嘛	མ
Yellow	Ni	呢	ཎི
Green	Pad	叭	པ
Blue	Me	嚩	དྨེ
Black	Hum	吽	ཧཱུྃ

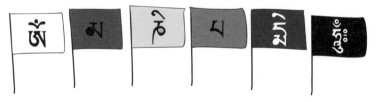

4.1 Six True Color Light Flags

Blessing Your Flags

The next step is to enhance the spiritual power of the flags using the Six True Words mantra. To begin this ritual, hold the white flag. Recite the syllable Om and blow on the flag, visualizing the blessing of the Buddhas infusing the flag. Visualize the power of the mantra permeating the flag and see the auspicious energy of the color white filling heaven and earth.

Repeat this process with the other five flags, blessing each one in turn. For the red flag, recite Ma and blow on the flag, seeing the color red. Similarly, for the yellow flag recite Ni, for the green flag recite Pad, for the blue flag recite Me, and for the black flag recite Hum.

Placing the Flags

Now you are ready to place your spiritually blessed flags in your environment. Arrange the flags in this order: white, red, yellow, green, blue, and black. This versatile cure has many applications. Here are some options:

To help your career
Place a set of six flags in any of these areas:

- On your desk in a cup holder or other container
- On the Wealth area of your desk
- In the Wealth area of your office at work
- In the Wealth area of your home office

To increase your wealth
Place the six flags in one or more locations:
- The Wealth area of your yard

- The Wealth area of your house
- The Wealth area of your bedroom

To improve your overall abundance
Place the flags so that they are visible when you enter the front door of your home.

THE TEN EMPERORS' COINS

The *Ten Emperors' Coins of the Qing Dynasty* are a powerful wealth cure that you can apply to your environment, or carry with you to adjust your qi for abundance. This cure represents the abundance of the treasuries of the ten Qing Dynasty Emperors (1644–1911), and holds powerful force for improving your financial position.

This cure consists of ten overlapping Chinese coins connected by a red cord, hung with a yellow cloth draped behind it (see Illustration 4.2). It contains one coin for each of the Ten Emperors of the Qing Dynasty, with Chinese characters written on each side. Place the coins so that the side with the most Chinese characters faces outward. Use either the large version of the coin cure, which is about four and a half feet in length, or the smaller travel size, which is about eleven inches long (for a source of these items, see Appendix). The coins in the larger version are about three inches in diameter.

Make sure you back the coins with the royal golden cloth that comes with them. The golden cloth is a key component of the cure, giving it power and support. Hang the coins vertically rather than horizontally, using the hanging loop provided for this purpose.

*4.2 Ten Emperors'
Qing Dynasty Coins*

You can place them in key locations to stimulate your abundance qi. One option is to place the coins so that they are immediately visible at the entrance of your home as soon as you open the door. This continual impression helps condition your qi for increased abundance.

You can also extend this cure to additional locations. Good choices include the entry to your master bedroom and the entry to your home office, or office at work. If you wish, you can frame this cure. This keeps others from touching it, which reduces its power. Another good placement is in the Wealth area of your home, bedroom, or office.

Ten Coins Travel Size

The travel-size Ten Emperors' Coins cure allows you to cultivate abundance qi wherever you go, whenever you need it. The cure fits in your pocket, purse, or briefcase. You can carry it in the small pouch it comes in, so that it stays clean and potent. Alternatively, you can place this cure in your desk drawer at home or at work, or under your pillow.

Good times to carry this cure with you include:

- When attending important business meetings or negotiations
- When making a key presentation, or attending a pressure-packed meeting
- When going to a court date or a meeting with your lawyer

However, you can carry it any time to boost abundance or increase your protection.

THE TWELVE ZODIAC ANIMALS

Making money usually involves some form of relationship. The Twelve Zodiac Animals help you improve your relationships with all of the twelve types of people represented by the twelve animals of Chinese mythology. This cure enhances your abundance by improving the quality of these relationships. There may be particular types of people with whom you don't get along. You need to engage positively with them or they can become blocks to your progress.

The Chinese calendar associates each year of birth with one of twelve animals. These are rat, ox, tiger, rabbit, dragon, snake, horse, ram, rooster, monkey, dog, and pig. The Twelve Zodiac Animals cure has golden miniatures of all twelve Chinese animals strung together vertically with a red string and backed by a red cloth (see Illustration 4.3). This potent tool helps smooth your interactions with associates, colleagues, and others.

To apply the cure, hang the Twelve Zodiac Animals at the entrance to your home or office so that they are easily visible as soon as you walk in. Additionally, you can place this cure in the front right area of your home or office, which is the Benefactors' area (see Illustration 4.4).

As with the Ten Emperors' Coins, the Twelve Zodiac Animals come in a smaller travel size that you can carry in your pocket, purse, or briefcase.

4.3 Twelve Zodiac Animals cure

POWERFUL SYMBOLS
NEAR YOUR ENTRANCE

Many Feng Shui cures are based on specific energetic symbols. They have a powerful effect if you place them appropriately with the correct motivation. In this section, I reveal two symbolic items that you can use to promote abundance and protect your home.

4.4 Twelve Zodiac Animals in Benefactors' Area

Buddha for Blessing

To bless your home for abundance, spiritual progress, and wisdom, place a small Buddha statue inside the house, in a position near the front door so that the Buddha faces it. The Buddha may be visible or invisible to the observer entering the house; both will be effective (see Illustration 4.5). The Buddha statue represents the enlightened being of the Buddha and of your own Buddha nature. It has significant power to help your home. The Buddha statue can be a very small one (one to two inches) and still be effective.

You can choose the aspect of Buddha that is closest to your heart: Buddha for wisdom; Quan Yin for compassion; Green Tara for healing. Or you can substitute a tiny figure of another deity from your own religion or faith. Place this cure with a pure motivation and a strong visualization.

Your Ship's Coming In

A powerful symbol of incoming prosperity is a boat positioned correctly in your space. This boat should be three-dimensional rather than a picture. Like the Buddha figure, the boat can be quite small (one to two inches). It should be placed inside the front door, with the bow pointed inward into the home—an important point (see Illustration 4.5). It symbolizes incoming wealth, abundance arriving, and your "ship coming in." If you place the boat with the bow pointed outward, you are telling abundance to "sail away." So make sure it's headed in the right direction! This boat can be

4.5 Ship and small Buddha cures in front entryway

any size and can be visible or placed in a hidden position in the front entry. (Putting a secondhand oil tanker in your front entry is probably overkill.)

Empowering Your Figurines

For best results, first place your chosen figurine on your altar or shrine for nine days. On each of these days, burn incense on the altar and pray with sincerity and intent in front of it. This process will infuse spiritual energy into the figurine, *and into you*, strongly enhancing the effectiveness of the cure. On the tenth day, place your charged figurine in its position near the front door.

CHAPTER
FIVE

Abundant Health

HEALTH IS A FUNDAMENTAL ingredient of true abundance. Having material abundance without enjoying vibrant health and vitality, or abundant qi, is like living in a well-painted house made of substandard materials. Qi fuels not only your body but also your emotional strength, your mental capabilities, and your capacity for joy. A truly happy person is filled with qi. When someone is "bubbling over" with joy, they are overflowing with positive qi. That's why we love to be around happy people; they are virtual fountains of qi, replenishing others wherever they go.

Asian philosophy holds that disease arises when qi is weak or out of balance. We are all bombarded with good advice for improving our physical health—to eat better, exercise more, reduce stress, and get more sleep. These outer measures are useful. But vibrant health involves an inner measure as well: nourishing the qi or vital energy circulating within our bodies. Just as Feng Shui nourishes the qi of your home and office to increase your financial abundance, energy exercises nourish your body's qi and give you abundant vitality and strength.

THE THREE TYPES OF HUMAN ENERGY

Ancient Asian traditions teach that the body has three "treasures" or key energies. These energies are stored in the body's three energy repositories or dan tiens (energy fields). The dan tiens are not physical organs. They are qi reservoirs, or energy storage tanks located within the body (see Illustration 5.1). When you are tired, sick, or depressed, your qi level is low. When you feel strong, vital, and confident, your qi level is high. Qi cultivation exercises increase your stores of these life energies, providing you with abundant fuel for life.

The three treasures are:

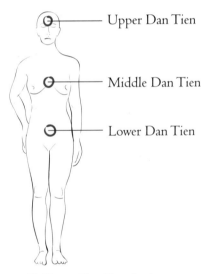

- *Jing:* raw primal or sexual energy. Your most basic life force, it is stored in the lower dan tien, located three finger widths below the navel, inside the body.
- *Qi:* basic life force. Basic qi, used in normal daily functioning—talking, moving, doing, is stored in the middle dan tien, located at the heart center.
- *Shen:* high-level spiritual force or energy. Shen, used in higher creativity, meditation, and subtle awareness, is stored in the upper dan tien, in the center of the head.

5.1 Upper, middle, and lower dan tiens

All three dan tiens are important. However, until you have practiced qi exercises extensively, focus on storing energy in the lower dan tien, below the navel. To facilitate this, rest your attention on this area while you perform qi exercises. Throughout this book, the term "dan tien" will refer to the lower dan tien.

SIXTEEN METHODS TO NOURISH YOUR HEALTH

There are many methods for enhancing your body's qi and improving your overall mind/body health. The sixteen exercises I give below are highly effective, yielding short- and long-term benefits, providing energetic nutrition in the moment, and increasing energy flow and mental clarity. It is not necessary to do them in order.

The Sixteen Methods

The best times for daily qi practice are in the morning shortly after arising, and in the evening before going to bed. However, any time is beneficial. I also recommend doing them at any point in the day if you need to replenish your energy.

The sixteen methods are divided into two parts: daily energy exercises and energy lifestyle recommendations. Perform the daily energy exercises in a set once a day if you can. And observe the energy lifestyle recommendations as you proceed through your day.

The methods are:

Daily Energy Exercises
- Combing the hair with the fingertips
- Uplifting the qi with fingers and palms
- Exercising the eyes regularly
- Beating the heavenly drum
- Biting front and rear teeth
- Swallowing saliva
- Uplifting the colon

- Breathing deeply with the abdomen
- Massaging the abdomen
- Using the joints regularly
- Rubbing soles of feet
- Dry washing the body (surface massage)
- Touching upper palate with tongue

Energy Lifestyle Tips
- Touching upper palate with tongue*
- Breathing deeply with the abdomen*
- Keeping your back warm at all times
- Keeping your chest protected at all times
- Avoiding talking while using the rest room

*I list "breathing with the abdomen" and "touching upper palate with tongue" in both sections because you benefit by doing them both in your daily exercise sequence and continuously throughout the day.

THE ENERGY EXERCISES

Combing the Hair with the Fingertips
This activity stimulates your scalp, increasing blood flow, brain activity, and alertness, and reduces tension and stress.

To perform this exercise:
Start by placing your fingertips at your forehead hairline, then rake or scratch backwards along your scalp with your fingernails (don't use an actual rake!), finish-

ing at the back of the neck (see
Illustration 5.2). Do nine repetitions with your left hand, covering
the entire scalp. Then do nine repetitions using your right hand.

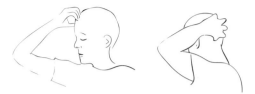

5.2 Combing the hair with the fingertips

This exercise is called "combing
the hair." But it really is more raking than combing. For best results, scratch your scalp
vigorously, but not so that it is painful, and certainly not hard enough to break the skin.

Uplifting Qi with Fingers and Palms

This method stimulates emotional and physical vitality and spiritual awareness by
"uplifting" your qi. The qi of a healthy, vital person flows upward from their feet
to their head and out to their fingers, much as a tree's energy surges up through its
branches into its leaves. When your qi flows up in this way you feel upright, strong,
and confident.

To perform this exercise:

Rub your palms together briskly until they grow warm and then rub them nine more
times. Rubbing your palms nine additional times after making them warm adds yang
energy, which according to Chinese energetics reaches its peak in multiples of nine.

Place your right palm on the center of your chest, fingers pointing upwards
toward your chin. Starting at the heart, lightly press the heel of your hand. While
inhaling through your nose, slide your hand upward, over the chest and the throat,
up and over the chin and the entire face and forehead. Press gently and smoothly
over the nose. When the heel of your palm reaches the top of your forehead,
shoot your hand vigorously upward to the full arm extension (see Illustration
5.3). As you shoot your hand up to arm's length above your head, exhale through

your nose and visualize your qi being strongly uplifted, flowing up your body and shooting out the top of your head.

This makes one repetition. Do nine repetitions with one hand; rub your hands again as before, and do nine with the other hand.

5.3   Uplifting the qi

Exercising the Eyes Regularly

Eye health is very important for mental alertness and clear thinking. We spend more and more time each day staring straight ahead at screens, screens, screens (TV, computer, video games). And we spend little time resting our eyes on beautiful healing scenes of nature (except those of us who use beautiful nature scenes as screen savers). Staring straight ahead, making only small movements, overly focuses the eyes on forward vision. It's as if we've put our eyes in tiny little straitjackets. This chronic focus and lack of full range of motion cause the eyes to lose flexibility, weakening the eye muscles, inhibiting broader movements, and affecting your vision. Over time, your eyes can become virtual couch potatoes.

But there are easy ways to improve the health of your eyes. The following exercises help restore the flexibility, strength, and health of your eye muscles, and can improve your vision. Do each exercise nine times, or as many times as is comfortable. Take care to never strain the eyes. Feel free to rest them anytime. If necessary, take several days to build up to nine repetitions.

To rest your eyes, try "palming." Rub your palms together until they are warm and then place them over your eyes for a minute. Do this several times to fully saturate your eyes with qi.

To perform this exercise:

Roll the eyes all the way around in a clockwise direction nine times.

Roll the eyes in the opposite direction nine times.

Move the eyes up and down nine times.

Move the eyes left to right nine times.

For extra improvement:

Move the eyes diagonally up to the right and down to the left nine times.

Move the eyes diagonally up to the left and down to the right nine times.

Move the eyes randomly nine times.

Beating the Heavenly Drum

Beating the Heavenly Drum energizes the brainstem area, producing a drumming sound that vibrates your entire head and brain. The gentle seal also benefits the ears.

This exercise improves your hearing and activates your brain, clearing thinking and memory. It stimulates the kidneys, which benefits your sex life and daily energy level. Better than a morning cup of coffee!

To perform this exercise:

Rub your palms together briskly until they are warm and then hot. Then place your palms gently over your ears and press firmly (but not hard), creating suction. Let your fingers rest on the back of your head and neck, pointing together, with your index fingers at the base of your skull and your thumbs resting on the side of your neck (see Illustration 5.4).

Now place your index fingers on top of your middle fingers. From this position, vigorously press your index fingers against the middle fingers and let them flick off quickly so that they strike the base of your skull. You will hear a resonant "drum-beat" resound in your skull. Do this alternately, flicking left and then right index fingers in rapid succession while listening to the internal drumming sound. Keep your palms pressed on your ears while flicking. Flick both index fingers against the base of your skull 9 or 27 times.

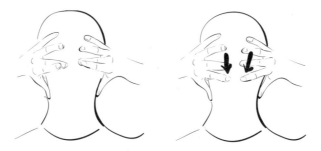

5.4 Beating the heavenly drum

Biting Front and Rear Teeth

Clicking the teeth calms the heart; it also enhances dental health, strengthening the teeth and gums, and helping tooth longevity. This practice also improves digestion and sexual vitality; best of all, it's free!

To perform this exercise:
Gently click your teeth together 27 times. For extra benefit, visualize your teeth, their roots, and your gums glowing with health.

Swallowing Saliva

Saliva, called "heavenly dew" by the Taoists, is a nourishing liquid when used appropriately. Some of the many benefits Taoist masters have discovered by swallowing saliva include nourishing the qi, conserving and recycling the body's energy, increasing vitality, and improving digestion, skin tone, and thyroid health.

To perform this exercise:

Gather your saliva and swish it from the front to the back of your tongue nine times. Now vigorously gulp down the saliva. Now swallow it, visualizing and feeling it sinking down to your dan tien.

Do the swish-and-swallow to the dan tien two more times. Perform this three times a day for a total of nine swallows. (Important note: Nine out of ten Taoist masters recommend that you only use your own saliva. We agree.)

Breathing Deeply with the Abdomen

Abdominal breathing is one of the best overall health practices. Breath is the foundation of life, yet most of us pay little if any attention to how we breathe. And most of us habitually breathe shallowly through the mouth into the upper chest. Shallow chest breathing brings less oxygen into your body, and reduces your intake of qi. Mouth breathing draws in unfiltered air, whereas the nostrils keep impurities from entering the lungs and the bloodstream. Take a moment to notice your own breathing. Are you breathing through your mouth or nose? Are you breathing more into your chest or your belly?

Abdominal breathing, also known as belly breathing, immediately increases your energy intake and creates a greater qi flow in your body. Breathing to the lower abdomen oxygenates the body, activating the parasympathetic nervous system, and massages the internal organs, releasing stress and tension. Babies naturally breathe this way before they pick up shallower chest breathing patterns from parents and society.

To perform this exercise:

Sit or stand comfortably, close your eyes, and relax your chest and abdomen. (Sitting with your back against a wall gives you kinesthetic feedback for this practice.) As you do this exercise, inhale and exhale through the nose while gently touching the roof of your mouth with your tongue.

Now relax your chest and breathe slowly, smoothly, and directly into your abdomen. Expand your belly to full capacity, gently expanding the sides of your abdomen, lower back, and kidney region. As your abdomen fills up, your chest will rise a little. But focus your attention on filling your belly with oxygen while keeping your chest relaxed. (It may help to place one hand on your chest and one on your belly at first.)

When your abdomen is full, retain the breath for five to ten seconds, as feels comfortable. This breath retention allows your body and blood to absorb more fresh oxygen, and release more toxins with the exhaled breath.

When you exhale, press your abdomen in to expel all the oxygen. Each in-breath brings in a full fresh supply of qi-filled oxygen. Each out-breath expels the used oxygen, which contains bodily toxins and wastes. Do this for several minutes and notice the sense of calmness and peace that results. Practice this daily until you can breathe naturally, expanding the belly while keeping the chest relaxed.

Start by performing nine consecutive abdominal breaths. Later increase to 18, and finally to 27 full breaths. A month of daily practice will retrain your body to breathe naturally into the abdomen. This new correct breathing habit will yield significant long-term health benefits.

Once you master the mechanical basics, you can increase the benefits of this exercise. As you breathe in, visualize radiant qi entering your body and passing through every cell on its way to your abdomen. With your abdomen full, continue to visualize the qi radiating throughout your entire body, your limbs, your hands and feet, your head and brain, stimulating and charging every cell, muscle, and organ in your body with life force.

Massaging the Abdomen

This exercise improves digestion, increases blood flow, and stimulates organ health.

Massaging the abdomen can relieve troublesome ailments such as indigestion, hypertension, and stomach dysfunction.

To perform this exercise:
Rub your palms together briskly until they are warm and then rub nine more times. Now place both your palms, one above the other, on your abdomen, fingertips pointed to the sides in opposite directions. Vigorously rub your hands from left to right across your abdomen, 9 or 27 times. Mentally see your organs as healthy, powerful, and filled with radiant qi. Now rub your hands again till warm, rub an additional nine times, and repeat the exercise, this time with top and bottom hands switched.

Uplifting the Colon
Squeezing and relaxing the anal sphincter muscle is an ancient yogic exercise that pumps qi throughout the entire body. Many of the body's energy meridians terminate at the anus. Therefore, contracting this area stimulates energy pathways that run throughout the body, creating many health benefits. It is beneficial for sexual health, counteracting urinary or bladder disorders, and even for healing hemorrhoids! (Don't worry, this exercise makes you less rather than more "anal.")

To perform this exercise:
Contract your anal sphincter muscle, keeping your stomach muscles as relaxed as possible. Perform this movement 9 or 27 times. You can inhale while contracting (using abdominal breathing) and exhale while relaxing. After practicing this method for a few weeks, you can increase its benefits by holding the contraction for up to five seconds before relaxing. Longer than this is not necessary. You can do this exercise sitting in a chair, on a couch, in your car, or standing in line.

Using the Joints Regularly

Whatever body part you exercise stays in better condition. The joints are no exception. Practicing full-range movement in your joints and limbs stimulates qi flow and helps reduce joint stiffness and pain.

To perform this exercise:

Exercise each joint 9 or 27 times, in the following order:

Wrists: Hold your arms in front of you, palms down, and make two fists. Now move your fists up and down as far as you can in both directions in a "knocking" motion.

Elbows: With your arms held straight out to your sides, palms facing up, slowly swing your hands in to your shoulders and back out again.

Shoulders: Start with your arms held straight out at your sides. Slowly swing them in, crossing in front of your chest and then swing them back out again. Stretch the shoulder joints in as full a range of motion as you can.

Ankles: Stand with your feet at shoulder width. Now lift one foot off the floor and rotate your foot and ankle in a complete circle nine times. Repeat with the other foot.

Knees: Stand with your feet together. You may want to balance yourself by holding on to a wall or a large piece of furniture. Bend your knee and swing the lower leg behind you as far as you can; try to bring your heel in contact with your buttock. Return it to its original position; perform this lift nine times. Lift the other knee in the same fashion.

Pelvis: Again here, you may want to balance yourself by holding on to a wall or a large piece of furniture. Standing on one leg, gently swing the other leg fully forward and backwards as far as it can go. Do nine leg swings and then swing the other leg.

Rubbing Soles of Feet

This practice stimulates the acupressure points of your feet, increases circulation, tones all your organs, stimulates vision and hearing, and improves overall health. This is because the soles connect to the meridians that run throughout the entire body.

To perform this exercise:

Rub your palms together briskly until they are warm, and then rub nine more times. With your right hand, rub the sole of your left foot vigorously 9 or 27 times. Rub hands as before, and rub the sole of your right foot vigorously with your left hand 9 or 27 times.

Dry Washing the Body: Surface Massage

Rubbing the body is a simple ancient exercise with many benefits. This exercise stimulates blood flow and qi to the skin, aiding circulation and health. It promotes youthfulness, helps improve kidney function, reduces stress, alleviates headaches, and improves the functioning of your immune system.

To perform this exercise:

Standing up, rub your palms together briskly until they are warm, and then an additional nine times.

Dry wash each of the following body parts nine times, rubbing them gently but firmly. After you rub each part, warm your hands and then rub them nine more times before moving on to the next part. Use the following sequence:

- Feet
- Shins and calves

- Thighs (front)
- Thighs (back)
- Pelvis, hips
- Torso (front)
- Torso (back)
- Arms
- Neck
- Face and head

THE LIFESTYLE METHODS

Touching Upper Palate with Tongue

Taoists teach that vital energy leaks from your body through your tongue, because of needless talking and poor "mouth posture." A slack or wagging tongue is a leaking qi hose. The simple solution is to touch your tongue comfortably to your upper palate, thereby recycling and stimulating your qi. This method also increases your body's production of saliva, which is quite beneficial.

To perform this exercise:
Place your tongue anywhere on your upper palate, without strain. Keep your tongue in this position as long as you can without discomfort.

Keep Your Back Warm at All Times; Keep Your Chest Protected at All Times

You may already observe these two basic health principles that can keep you from getting a cold. A cold can zap your energy for days or weeks and can lead to conditions that are more serious.

To perform this exercise:

Pay attention to the environment and weather. Don't let your back or your chest get cold or wet, especially in cool weather. If they do, change clothes as quickly as possible. Wear sufficient outerwear or a scarf if needed.

Avoid Talking When Using the Rest Room

Remember the part about losing energy from your tongue? Qigong masters say using the rest room does the same thing; therefore, they recommend not talking while eliminating. Those important cell phone calls will just have to wait!

Like all the techniques in this book, the Sixteen Methods to Nourish Your Health cannot replace common sense, proper diet and exercise, or professional medical advice. Rather, they provide you with a simple recipe to maintain your qi and increase your personal energy.

CHAPTER
SIX

Meditation to Increase Your Abundance

IN TRADITIONAL CHINESE medicine your qi, or life force, is the essence of who you are. Your body is simply the vehicle for your qi. Outer Feng Shui methods align, balance, and increase the qi of your physical environments—your living and working spaces. They transform *where* you are. Inner Feng Shui methods align, balance, and increase the qi of your inner environment. They transform *who* you are. Using both outer and inner Feng Shui delivers the most benefits, increasing your personal qi and your abundance. Meditation is a principal inner method of qi cultivation.

The Meditation to Establish the Foundation helps strengthen your personal, financial, and spiritual qi. It sets the stage for additional meditation methods.

This meditation is beneficial at any time of the day. However, meditation in the morning after waking and at night before going to bed is highly recommended. Morning meditation aligns and uplifts your mental and spiritual qi and prepares you for the day. Evening meditation brings inner peace and allows your sleep to be deeper and more rejuvenating for mind, body, and spirit.

For best results, make a commitment to do this meditation in the morning and in the evening every day for 27 days. If you do it at least once a day, you will notice benefits.

Find a place where you can sit comfortably without distractions. If you can, set up an altar with images or objects that have personal spiritual meaning, or that honor a deity of your religion. This altar should also feature a lamp with a red bulb. Otherwise, you can visualize such an altar in your mind.

This meditation is on the companion audio CD. Try meditating with the CD several times until you internalize the meditation so that you can do it on your own.

MEDITATION TO ESTABLISH THE FOUNDATION

Calming Yourself
Take your most relaxed and comfortable sitting position. Sit in front of the altar with the red bulb or visualize that you are doing so. Take a moment to relax yourself and calm your mind. Feel yourself becoming more and more relaxed, calm, and clear. Place your hands in the Heart-Calming Mudra, palms facing up with the left hand on top of the right, and the thumb tips touching.

Close your eyes and silently recite the Heart-Calming Mantra nine times: *Gate Gate, Para Gate, Para Sum Gate, Bodhi Swaha.* (You can hear the correct pronunciation on the CD.)

Visualize that everything in the universe is still, and all is emptiness. Now, tightly close your eyes. Then suddenly open them and stare at the red lamp on the altar table, trying not to blink. Then close your eyes lightly, or keep them half open.

Swaying the Body
Visualize a line going from your perineum (the space between your anus and genitals) to your crown chakra—the "vertical axis" of your body.

Sway your body to the left and right
Using this axis, sway your body to the left and to the right nine times (see Illustration

6.1). Sway anywhere from a few inches to a foot to each side. One cycle to the left and right equals one repetition. Visualize that all your physical pain and illnesses are shaken off with the swaying motions.

6.1 Swaying body left and right

Sway your body to the front and back
Now sway your body front and back nine times. Visualize that mental and emotional attachments—grief, fear, anger, sadness—are all shaken off with your swaying motions, along with negative karma from past, present, and future lifetimes.

Rotate your body clockwise
Starting from the left side, rotate your body clockwise nine times (see Illustration 6.2). Visualize that with the help of external forces, tens of thousands of Buddhas' lights are shining onto you, and into your body. Visualize the Buddhas' lights pen-

etrating your body, so that every part, from head to toe—even your fingertips, teeth, and every strand of hair—are shining with the Buddhas' lights.

6.2 *Rotating body clockwise*

Rotate your body counterclockwise
Starting from the right side, rotate your body counterclockwise nine times (see Illustration 6.3). Visualize that with the help of internal forces, your meditation Buddha appears at your heart, giving you a clear conscience and peace of mind. Your meditation Buddha's light emanates and fills your entire body, so that every part of your body from head to toe is filled and shining with the Buddha's light.

6.3 *Rotating body counter-clockwise*

MAKING WISHES IN YOUR HEART

Do the following visualizations to create abundance in desired areas of your life.

Asking for Wealth

Visualize the Ten Emperors' Coins of the Qing Dynasty circulating inside your body increasing your abundance as follows (see Illustration 6.4):

- The coins circulate inside your feet, so that wherever you stand, there is wealth.
- They circulate inside your hands, so you receive more wealth through your hands.
- They circulate inside your head, so your thoughts continuously create more abundance.

- They circulate inside your heart, so that your intentions bring you more wealth.
- They circulate inside your limbs, so that your actions create more wealth.

Asking for Spiritual Development

Visualize that the six sounds of the Six True Words Mantra (Om, Ma, Ni, Pad, Me, and Hum) are circulating inside your entire body increasing your spiritual power. Hear each sound circulating inside (see Illustration 6.5). This process aids your spiritual progress. In addition to hearing the sounds circulating, also see the colors of the mantra syllables inside your body as follows:

- When you hear the sound Om circulating, see the color white circulating with the sound.
- When you hear the sound Ma circulating, see the color red.
- When you hear the sound Ni circulating, see the color yellow.
- When you hear the sound Pad circulating, see the color green.
- When you hear the sound Me circulating, see the color blue.
- When you hear the sound Hum circulating, see the color black.

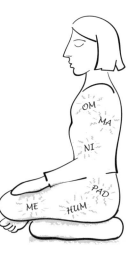

6.4 *Circulating the Ten Emperors' coins*

6.5 *Circulating the Six True sounds*

Asking for Enhancement of Your Qi

Inhale, visualizing light beginning at your feet, traveling smoothly up to your eyebrows in five continuous stages without exhaling. On the sixth stage, exhale, seeing the light shooting out the top of your head. As you breathe, mentally hear the sounds of the Six True Words mantra and visualize the associated six colors as follows:

- Inhale, visualizing white light traveling from the soles of your feet up to your knees, hearing the sound Om.
- Inhale red light from your knees up to your hips, hearing the sound Ma.
- Inhale yellow light from your hips up to your navel, hearing the sound Ni.
- Inhale green light starting from your navel, filling up your torso, arms, and hands up to your neckline, hearing the sound Pad.
- Inhale blue light from your neck up to your eyebrow level, hearing the sound Me.
- Now exhale black light from your eyebrows shooting out of your crown to infinity, hearing the sound Hum.

Do the above sequence three or nine times.

Dedicating the Merit

An eight-petaled pink lotus blossoms in your heart. On top of this lotus appears your meditation Buddha. The Buddha expands step by step to fill up your whole body. You are now one with the Buddha; you are the Buddha, and the Buddha is you. You are filled with Buddha's golden light.

Your golden light blesses countless Buddhas and spiritual beings that surround you in all directions. Your light enters them and blesses them thoroughly. The light of the Buddhas shines to you in return, filling you up and blessing you thoroughly.

Visualize yourself exchanging spiritual light and blessing with all sentient beings.

Visualize sending golden light to your spiritual teacher and receiving golden light from him or her.

Now send light to your family, friends, and loved ones, and receive blessings from them in return.

Send Buddha's light to bless your home, workplace, and automobile. Visualize the light returning to your body.

Make a wish for your life in whatever area you choose: increased prosperity, better health, success in your career, improved relationships, or anything else you desire.

Hold the Heart-Calming Mudra; recite the Six True Words Mantra nine times: Om Ma Ni Pad Me Hum.

For the four active segments of this meditation, as heard on Track 2 of the accompanying CD, I lead you in the first repetition of each exercise and provide silence for you to complete eight additional repetitions.

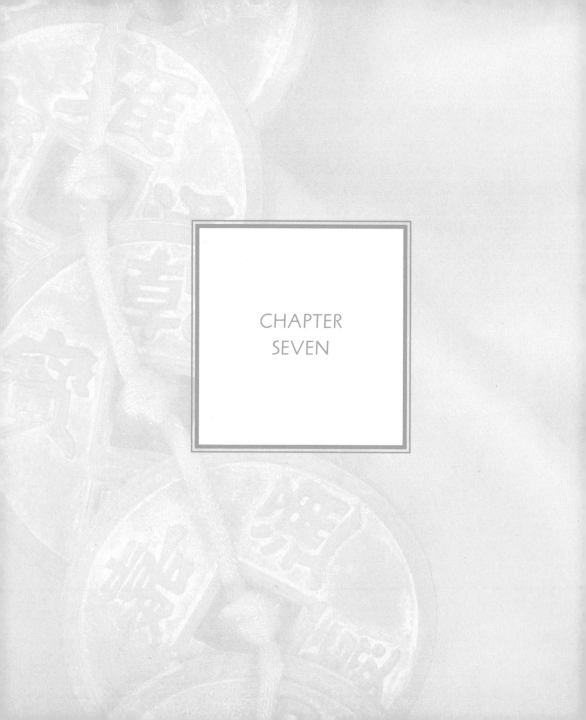

CHAPTER SEVEN

Meditation to Bless Your Life in Every Area

SPIRITUAL TECHNIQUES and cures hold the highest rank in Feng Shui. Spiritual Feng Shui is potent because you are directly enhancing the qi of your environment, your body, and your mind at the same time.

The Activation of the Spiritual Power of the Eight Trigrams Meditation is a secret method taught by Grandmaster Lin Yun Rinpoche. The greatest benefits come when you perform this meditation on a daily basis with a sincere heart. This meditation is also on the companion CD so that you can practice and gradually master the method.

This meditation helps you improve your abundance in all areas of life, including:

- Your money
- Your love life
- Your health and your mental, emotional, and spiritual well-being
- Your family harmony, happiness, and balance

While meditating, you will visualize yourself standing at the entrance of your home or bedroom, looking in. You will visualize projecting energy patterns in the form of trigrams (powerful three-line patterns) onto eight key areas of your home's perimeter. These are the eight areas of the Ba-Gua (see Chapter 1). Then you will visualize highly accomplished masters ("immortals") emerging from these areas and blessing you. They provide immense benefits for your well-being. If you wish, you can instead visualize angels or saints blessing you, in alignment with your beliefs.

THE ACTIVATION OF THE SPIRITUAL POWER OF THE EIGHT TRIGRAMS MEDITATION

Calming Your Mind

To begin the Eight Trigrams Meditation, first assume a comfortable and natural position, sitting, standing, or lying down. Relax yourself and calm your mind. Place your hands in your lap. Slow your breathing, and allow your chest, stomach, arms, and legs to relax. Let all the tension drain out of your body and mind, like a rope gradually untwisting and freeing itself. You are feeling very peaceful and relaxed.

Hold the Heart-Calming Mudra (sacred hand gesture): hands facing up, left hand on top of right, with the thumbs touching (see Chapter 8), and recite the Heart-Calming Mantra nine times: *Gate Gate, Para Gate, Para Sum Gate, Bodhi Swaha.* (You can hear the correct pronunciation of this mantra on the companion CD.) Visualize everything dissolving into a void; you are becoming one with the whole universe.

Receiving Blessing

Visualize yourself standing in the doorway of your house or bedroom. An eight-petaled pink lotus blossoms at your heart. On this lotus is your own meditation Buddha or your personal deity. Your Buddha or deity gradually expands until it completely fills your body. You are one with the Buddha, and the Buddha is one with you.

Your whole body is filled with the light of the Buddha. Visualize that you now have three eyes instead of two. Your third eye is located between your eyebrows, stands oriented vertically on your forehead, and is wide open (see Illustration 7.1).

In the distance, you hear the sound *Hung*. It approaches gradually, and as it gets closer, it becomes louder and louder. It enters your body through your third eye and becomes a small white ball. The ball travels down to the dan tien, three finger widths below your navel and inside your body. The white ball turns golden and swirls up to your three eyes. All three of your eyes are golden in color, and radiating powerful beams of golden light. Visualize your three golden eyes projecting three rays of golden light, shining on the following areas of your home in turn.

Family area: the left-hand center part of your home or room

Visualize the three rays of golden light from your three golden eyes writing ☳, the Jen trigram, on the wall in the Family area of your home or room. The lines on the wall are golden, vibrating with energy, and radiating golden light.

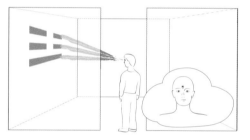

7.1 *Writing Trigram on the Family area wall with light beams*

Now visualize a wise and powerful immortal gradually emerging from the wall, dressed in a blue Chinese robe. On the robe is the Jen trigram pattern in shining gold.

Visualize this immortal walking toward you and telling you about your family's well-being. The immortal blesses the safety and fortune of your family, protecting you, improving your family relationships, and creating harmony. Your whole family is blessed, safe, and protected.

The immortal returns to the Family area wall and gradually disappears into it.

Wealth area: the back left part of your home or room

Visualize the three rays of golden light from your three golden eyes writing 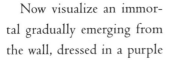, the Hsun trigram, on the wall in the Wealth area of your home or room. The lines on the wall are golden, vibrating with energy, and radiating golden light.

Now visualize an immortal gradually emerging from the wall, dressed in a purple

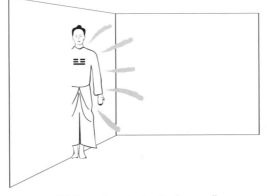

7.2 *Immortal emerging from Family area wall*

Chinese robe. On the robe is the Hsun trigram in shining gold. The immortal comes toward you bearing valuables, money, and treasures. This being delivers all this wealth to you, and blesses you so that more fortune can come to your home. You see your wishes for wealth coming true in detail.

The immortal returns to the Wealth area wall and gradually disappears into it.

Fame and Reputation: the back center part of your home or room

Visualize the three rays of golden light from your three golden eyes writing 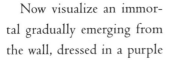, the Li trigram, on the wall in the Fame area of your home or room. The lines on the wall are golden, vibrating with energy, and radiating golden light.

Visualize an immortal gradually emerging from the wall, dressed in a red Chinese robe. On the robe is the Li trigram in shining gold. The immortal hangs a wind chime in the back center area of your home or bedroom and rings the chime, blessing your fame and improving your reputation. You see your reputation as positive and enhanced, and your path to fame progressing smoothly.

The immortal returns to the Fame area wall and gradually disappears into it.

Marriage area: the back right part of your home or room

Visualize the three rays of golden light from your three golden eyes writing ☷, the Kun trigram, on the wall in the Marriage area of your home or room. The lines on the wall are golden, vibrating with energy, and radiating golden light.

Now see an immortal gradually emerging from the wall dressed in a pink Chinese robe. On the robe is the Kun trigram in shining gold. The immortal blesses the well-being of your mother, sisters, daughters, and all the female members of the family. If you have any difficulties in your marriage or relationship, the immortal resolves the problems and difficulties, creating a happy marriage. If you desire a relationship, visualize the immortal matching you with "Mr." or "Ms. Right." The female members of your family and your relationship or marriage are greatly blessed.

The immortal returns to the Marriage area wall and gradually disappears into it.

Children area: the center right-hand side of your home or room

Visualize the three rays of golden light from your three golden eyes writing ☱, the Tui trigram, on the wall in the Children area of your home or room. The lines on the wall are golden, vibrating with energy, and radiating golden light.

Visualize an immortal gradually emerging from the wall dressed in a white Chinese robe. On the robe is the Tui trigram in shining gold.

The immortal expands the wisdom of your children and their offspring, blessing them with safety and health, a smooth and progressive education, and successful careers. If any of your children has an ailment, the immortal heals them and enhances their qi flow. All your children are protected, healthy, and safe.

The immortal returns to the Children area wall and gradually disappears into it.

Benefactors area: the front right-hand part of your home or room

Visualize the three rays of golden light from your three golden eyes writing ☰, the Chien trigram, on the wall in the Benefactors area of your home or room. The lines on the wall are golden, vibrating with energy, and radiating golden light.

Now see an immortal gradually emerging from the wall, dressed in a gray Chinese robe. On the robe is the Chien trigram in shining gold. The immortal is resolving problems faced by your husband, father, brothers, sons, and the male members of your family. The immortal gives you protective blessings to avoid all harm and accidents when you travel. The being blesses you so people give you assistance in all areas of life.

The immortal returns to the Benefactors area wall and gradually disappears into it.

Career area: the front center part of your home or room

Visualize the three rays of golden light from your three golden eyes writing ☵, the Kan trigram, on the wall in the Career area of your home or room. The lines on the wall are golden, vibrating with energy, and radiating golden light.

Visualize an immortal gradually emerging from the wall, dressed in a black Chinese robe. On the robe is the Kan trigram in shining gold. The immortal blesses your career, resolving all difficulties and obstructions. Your career, if not going smoothly, will improve and you will prosper. If you need a new work opportunity, the immortal introduces you to all the right contacts.

The immortal returns to the Career area wall and gradually disappears into it.

Self-Cultivation: the left-hand front part of your home or room

Visualize the three rays of golden light from your three golden eyes writing ☶, the Ken trigram, on the wall in the Self-Cultivation area of your home or room. The lines on the wall are golden, vibrating with energy, and radiating golden light.

See an immortal gradually emerging from the wall, dressed in a midnight blue Chinese robe. On the robe is the Ken trigram in shining gold.

The immortal places a hand on your crown and blesses you with spiritual energy, opening the wisdom center of your brain and elevating your spiritual level. The immortal helps increase the wisdom, knowledge, and spiritual cultivation of everyone in your home. Your intuition, personal growth, and spiritual maturity are all enhanced.

The immortal returns to the Self-Cultivation area wall and gradually disappears into it.

Unified Blessings

Visualize a large Tai Chi diagram ☯ appearing in the center of your eight-times activated and blessed home or bedroom. Visualize the eight immortals standing at their respective positions around the diagram (see Illustration 7.3). They now approach you to bless you all at once. Then they return to their respective areas, reinforcing and enhancing your house and your life with their powers. Each area is blessed and vibrates with strong, positive energy.

7.3 *Eight immortals giving blessings*

Sharing the Energy

Visualize an eight-petaled pink lotus blossoming in your heart. In its center is a golden Buddha.

The Buddha steadily grows within you until it fills you completely. Now your head is full of the Buddha's perfect wisdom; your heart is full of the Buddha's great compassion; your arms and legs are full of the Buddha's infinite power. You are one with the Buddha, and the Buddha is one with you. You and the Buddha are one entity. The Buddha's light fills you up and shines onto:

- The myriad Buddhas in the universe. Their blessing light shines back to you in turn.
- All beings in the universe, raising them from suffering to happiness to ultimate peace. Their blessing light shines back to you in turn.
- Your spiritual teacher or the person who helps you most spiritually. His or her blessing light shines back to you in turn.
- Friends and relatives. Their blessing light shines back to you in turn.
- Your home and office, clearing any negative and bad luck qi and filling it with auspicious qi and blessings.

Your blessing light returns to your body.

Completion
Make a wish for whatever you desire, and while holding the Heart-Calming Mudra (see page 62) repeat the Six True words Mantra, *Om Mani Padme Hum*, nine times.

Tracking Your Progress
Don't expect to master this meditation the first time through. It will take time to perfect it. However, its benefits justify the dedication you put into it. Keep up your efforts and you will improve steadily. Practice and persistence is the path to performing this preeminent practice with precision and panache.

Secret Meditation

The Activation of the Spiritual Power of the Eight Trigrams Meditation is a secret method of Black Sect Tantric Buddhism taught by Grandmaster Lin Yun Rinpoche. Everyone is now welcome to read it if they wish. However, if you teach this meditation, or the one given in the previous chapter, to another, the red envelope tradition applies. Use spiritual discrimination, share only if a very sincere person requests it (not with someone that you suggest it to), and share it only with a person who presents you with 27 red envelopes, each containing money, traditionally $10 in each envelope.

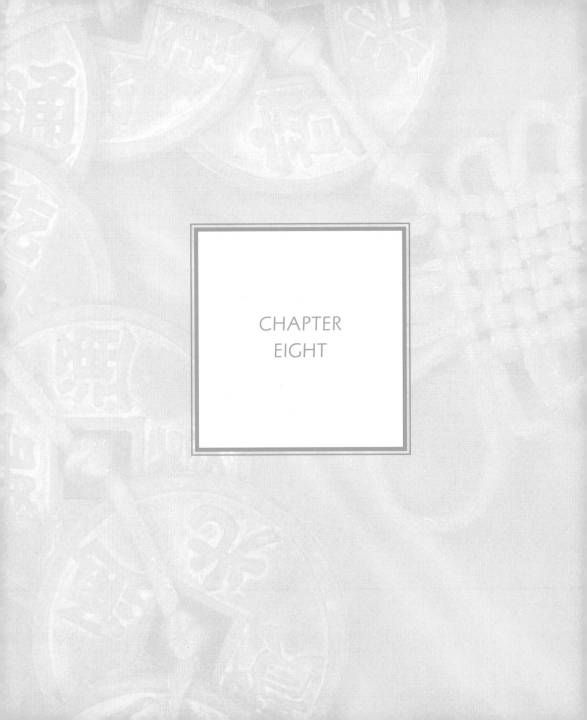

CHAPTER
EIGHT

Spiritual Aspects of Abundance Feng Shui

THIS CHAPTER GIVES YOU vital insights into powerful aspects of qi cultivation. The Three Secret Reinforcement is an essential part of your cures that applies spiritual power to your physical Feng Shui changes. We also discuss some of the result patterns you can expect with Feng Shui, timing your cures, and the value of keeping cure details within your household.

THREE SECRETS REINFORCEMENT

One of the essential techniques of Grandmaster Lin Yun's Feng Shui method is to reinforce your cures with spiritual power. The Three Secrets Reinforcement uses three areas of life (body, speech, and mind) to empower your intention, visualize your desires, and connect to the qi of the cure. Using both yang and yin energies in your cures makes them more effective. The yang, or visible, portion of the cure is done by making a change in your environment. The Reinforcement is the yin, or invisible, portion of the cure. Although I give you the tools to perform the

Reinforcement, you will also find it beneficial to receive personal instruction on this technique from a qualified Feng Shui teacher.

The Three Secrets Reinforcement is a vital part of each cure, as it brings the power of both human and divine qi into it. Combining these with beneficial placement greatly enhances the power of the cure. Cures performed without using the Reinforcement are significantly less effective.

The Reinforcement uses three vehicles to reinforce your Feng Shui cures. Body is the vehicle of action and manifestation. The *body secret* is the use of mudras, or sacred hand gestures. Speech is the vehicle of communication. The *speech secret* is the use of mantras, or spiritual invocation. Mind is the vehicle of transformation. The *mind secret* is the use of visualization, or seeing the desired results in your mind's eye.

THE BODY SECRET IS MUDRA

The first step of the Reinforcement is the body secret. The body secret spiritually aligns the body, allowing positive, healing energy to flow into your life. A mudra is a body position or sacred hand gesture that creates uplifting or divine feelings.

Eastern traditions have many hand mudras, each producing different energetic effects by aligning, balancing, and harmonizing the qi, which terminates in the fingertips. Mudras have a powerful effect on your body and mind. Placing your fingers in specific patterns tunes your energy to specific frequencies that are gateways to heightened states of consciousness. Mudras involving movement, whether hand gestures or physical postures, yield best results when repeated nine times. You only need one mudra for each Reinforcement. Choose the one that feels most comfortable for you.

Expelling Mudra

A common mudra for the Three Secrets is the "expelling gesture," which involves flicking the second and third fingers out from the palm. This mudra involves motion, which triggers action. It expels negativity and infuses positive qi into your space. Point your forefinger and pinky outward and hold down the ring and middle fingers with your thumb. Then simultaneously flick ring and middle fingers outward nine times in a row. (Women use the right hand and men the left hand.)

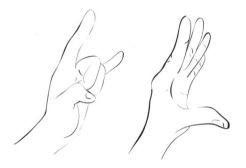

8.1 The Expelling Mudra

Heart-Calming Mudra

The Heart-Calming Mudra calms the heart and the mind. For this simple mudra, you make a bowl with your hands, the left hand on top and the thumbs touching. (Men and women perform this mudra the same way.)

8.2 The Heart-Calming Mudra

Sword Mudra

This mudra is a powerful method for protection and safety. Place your palms together, interlace your fingers, and point your first two fingers forward (see Illustration 8.3). Simply hold this position while you recite the mantra and visualize your desired result. Your thumbs point upward. Be sure to point with two fingers rather than one, which is ineffective.

8.3 The Sword Mudra

THE SPEECH SECRET IS MANTRA

The second step of your Reinforcement is the speech secret, the reciting of mantras or invocations. With the speech secret you use the power of the spoken word to invoke your intentions and help them manifest. It is recommended that you recite the mantra nine times.

Mantras are sacred words whose vibrations conduct spiritual power. When you chant a mantra, you invoke a specific energy and access a corresponding state of consciousness. Your inner motivation or spiritual attitude in chanting a mantra significantly affects the results produced by the mantra. Therefore, always say mantras with sincerity and devotion.

In your Reinforcements, you can choose from the mantras I give below, or use sacred speech (such as prayers or chants) from your personal religious tradition.

The Six True Words Mantra

Om Mani Padme Hum (ohm MAH-nee PAHD-mee HOOM)

This mantra is the Six True Words, or Mantra of Compassion. It means, "Hail to the Jewel in the Lotus." Its benefits include healing from mental and physical disease, protection for you and your family, improvement to your spiritual growth, and the fulfillment of your wishes.

The Heart-Calming Mantra

Gate, Gate Para Gate Para Sam Gate Bodhi Swaha (GAH-tay, GAH-tay, PAHR-uh GAH-tay, PAHR-uh sum GAH-tay, BOH-dee, SWA-ha)

Repeating this mantra calms the body and the mind. It helps create peace if you are overly energized. It connects to the essence of enlightenment.

The Green Tara Mantra

Om Tare Tu Tare Ture Swaha (Om TAH-ray TOO TAH-ray TOOR-ree SO-ha)

Reciting this mantra is helpful for protection, assistance, and healing. It connects to Green Tara, the goddess of compassion and healing, also known as the mother of the Buddhas. Her green color represents healing.

The Lord Tonpa Shenrab Mantra

Om Ma Tri Mu Ye Sa Le Du (om MAH-tri MOO-yee SAH-ley Doo)

This important mantra is the highest mantra in Grandmaster Lin Yun's teachings. It helps dissolve negative emotions and invokes in you the positive and pure qualities of love, generosity, wisdom, openness, peacefulness, and compassion. It connects to the founder of Black Sect Tantric Buddhism, Lord Tonpa Shenrab. An enlightened figure who lived 18,000 years ago, he founded the Bon religion of Tibet, which predates Buddhism. His position is similar to that of Shakyamuni Buddha in Buddhism.

THE MIND SECRET IS VISUALIZATION

The third and final step of the process utilizes the mind. The mind secret, which uses *visualization* to empower your intentions, is very effective for achieving your goals. During this step, you can visualize the abundance and wealth you desire coming into your life.

A Feng Shui cure has a physical and a spiritual component. Of these two, the spiritual is the stronger. Of the Three Secrets, the mind secret, or visualization, is the most powerful. The strength of your visualization is a key factor in the success of your cures. You will find it worthwhile to improve your visualization ability through meditation, and cultivate your spirituality in general.

GETTING RESULTS WITH YOUR CURES

Results from Feng Shui are different for everyone, just as with diet or exercise. Results from your cures depend on these three factors: your life pattern and personal qi; the nature of the problem and the details of your situation; and the appropriateness of the applied cures and the skill and sincerity with which they are applied.

Feng Shui results occur when cures improve the energy flow in your environment, which in turn improves your personal energy. Results vary based on the above factors. Here are some of the different ways I have noticed that results take effect in people's lives after they apply proper solutions:

- Sudden, easy, positive results (what we all wish for)
- Sudden, intense, transformational results (what we sometimes get instead)
- Slow, gradual improvement
- A delay, followed by a sudden "boost" in life

Always visualize your desired results, but don't be overly attached to the specific outcomes you've imagined. You may get a result that closely matches your visualization, or a different, unexpected result that is as good or even better than what you imagined. Be sure to watch for the changes you desire and notice when they arrive.

IMPECCABLE TIMING

To increase your odds of success, you can perform cures during two powerful Feng Shui time spans. These two "zones" are between 11:00 a.m. and 1:00 p.m. (daytime), when cosmic energies are changing from yin to yang; and between 11:00 p.m. and 1:00 a.m. (nighttime), when they're shifting from yang to yin. The transformational energy in these times adds extra power to your cures.

Timing is just icing on the cake for your cures, not a requirement. If you can't do a cure during these times, do it as soon as you can.

THE RED ENVELOPE TRADITION

Grandmaster Lin Yun teaches that red envelopes should be given to one who provides:

- A formal Feng Shui consultation
- An informal consultation, or tips to a friend
- A Feng Shui class

Giving red envelopes containing monetary offerings honors the knowledge and energy of Feng Shui and is important for the safety of the person transmitting the cures. It also shows sincere gratitude to the giver for the knowledge obtained. The envelopes can be of any size as long as they are red in color and have not been used for another purpose. Give one or more for each cure you receive, or a multiple of nine envelopes.

SHARING FENG SHUI KNOWLEDGE

Once they discover Feng Shui, many people are tempted to go on an evangelistic crusade to improve the lives of everyone they know. I advise care and wisdom, rather than boldness here. Giving out cures without proper precautions and training can make the situation worse rather than better.

Doing your own Feng Shui is like taking better care of your own health; there are many benefits to receive. However, caring for your body does not make you a trained doctor. Prescribing Feng Shui cures for others is a big responsibility. I recommend undertaking it only if you are formally trained as a practitioner.

KEY POINTS ON DISCUSSING CURES

According to Grandmaster Lin's teachings, for the safety and protection of all involved, giving Feng Shui cures, tips, and teachings should occurs only when all of these criteria are met:

- The giver has the appropriate professional Feng Shui training.
- Cures are requested and are appropriate to the situation.
- The red envelopes tradition is honored: The receiver of the sacred knowledge gives red envelopes containing monetary offerings to the one providing the cures or instruction.

In addition, keep the intentions and details of each of your own Feng Shui cures private to help maintain the momentum created by your cures. Sharing the particulars of your cures with others can reduce their results. Strange but true.

CHAPTER NINE

Living the Abundant Life

FENG SHUI IS an important aspect of your plan for creating abundance, but it is only one part. Rearranging your environment alone won't necessarily produce powerful Feng Shui results. Physical Feng Shui methods by themselves do not magically solve your problems. A corresponding inner change or adjustment is often required. If you focus solely on physical methods and ignore the critical inner components, you may transfer problems from one area of life to another, prolonging complications and postponing real solutions. And your unaddressed problems may creep up on you in unexpected ways. In addition to the Feng Shui techniques that I've described, two important pathways to abundance are gratitude and generosity.

GRATITUDE

Giving thanks for what you have is a key practice. Appreciating and enjoying your blessings open up your energy field for more good to flow to you. Grumbling, complaining, and feeling negative about your life shut off the inflow quicker than a kink in a garden hose.

Being thankful for what you have helps you enjoy life and reduces your craving for more, more, more. We need a measure of wealth to live in today's society; money is involved in most of our everyday transactions. However, material items cannot give us happiness; at best, they temporarily satisfy us but, like empty calories, they do not nourish us.

GENEROSITY

When we look at life from the standpoint of karma, we realize that the level of abundance we are experiencing today is the result of our actions, thoughts, and words in the past. Therefore, the abundance we will experience in the future comes from our actions today.

Spiritually speaking, the most powerful long-term strategy to increase your abundance is to increase your generosity. When you are generous with others, you create abundance for yourself in the future. You store up powerful vibrations in your energy field that manifest as more abundance in your future.

Remember that abundance of your heart is just as important as abundance of your pocketbook. Constantly thinking about yourself, what you want, and how to meet your immediate needs keeps you from seeing life's bigger picture. Giving to others helps remove the focus from obsessing on your problems and opens and expands your heart. It gives you the joy that results from making others happy.

So, practice generosity as much as possible. Keep in mind that even tiny acts of generosity are very effective for increasing your own abundance, especially when you perform them with a strong motivation to help others.

ABUNDANT MIND, ABUNDANT ENERGY

Another key factor is to learn to think in an abundant way. Money is not a savior; it is neither a path to happiness nor an evil we are better off without. Instead, money is a neutral energy, and we have as much of it as our energy field allows. This energy field consists of our personal energy plus our environmental energy. Using this book, you will improve both areas. Meditation and qi cultivation help your personal energy field; Feng Shui changes improve your environmental energy field. The best results come from utilizing both approaches. It is vital to use both mundane and spiritual methods of gaining abundance to maximize your chances of achieving prosperity and wholeness.

FENG SHUI WORKS

My wish is for you to experience increased abundance at many different levels—in your physical environment, relationships, and your spiritual life. I trust that this learning program has provided you with the tools you need to create the life changes you desire.

Feng Shui can deliver genuine shifts in your home, environment, and the total quality of your life. In my own life, implementing the spiritual aspects of Feng Shui has resulted in greater peace, abundance, and clarity, as well as increasing insight as to which cures are the most appropriate for the situations I face. I believe that you will experience similar if not greater benefits.

Here are some important characteristics to check for when acquiring the tools mentioned in this book. Select the highest quality when choosing items that you will implement as Feng Shui cures.

FACETED CRYSTAL SPHERES

Crystal spheres are faceted (not smooth) leaded glass spheres; the best known are made by Swarovski in Austria. A high-quality faceted crystal creates rainbow prisms when exposed to sunlight. The color spectrum created by the sphere should be vibrant, crisp, and clear. I recommended using spheres that are 40 mm (about 1 1/2 in.), 50 mm (about 2 in.), or 60 mm (about 2 1/3 in.) in diameter. You can find these at local stores or on the Internet; many stores carry them for Feng Shui purposes.

WIND CHIMES

When using wind chimes for Feng Shui purposes, the essential factor is their sound quality. An effective chime has a resonant ringing sound that is clear, lasting, and vibratory. The sound continues to resonate after you strike the chime. This is why metal chimes are best; brass is a good metal, but pay more attention to the sound than the type of metal. The chimes' sound should be pleasing. The number of chime rods or tubes, or whether they are solid or hollow, is your choice.

BAMBOO FLUTES

Characteristics of good flutes for your cures are threefold. First, their bamboo segment ridges should be intact; a flute with its ridges sanded off gives almost no benefit. The flute's bamboo segments should increase in length along the distance of the flute (see Illustration 2.5). Lastly, your chosen flute ideally should be one that was designed as a sacred object and has not been played with or handled roughly. I recommend Feng Shui flutes from one source, which abides by these standards; see "To Order" below for details.

MOBILES

The movement created by mobiles activates qi in the environment. They circulate energy gracefully and continuously within their space. Choose the highest quality mobile you can afford: one that is relatively silent and of good craftsmanship. You will obtain greater benefits and enjoyment from one that has been thoughtfully crafted.

RED RIBBON

• Use a red ribbon, cord, or string to hang the above cures. Depending upon the cure and where you are hanging it, your ribbon could be any multiple of nine inches (27, 54, 108 inches).

TO ORDER

Many of the cures recommended are available from the Yun Lin Temple, a non-profit organization dedicated to teaching Feng Shui and Buddhist methods. These cures include:

- 10 Emperors' Coins
- 12 Zodiac Animals
- Bamboo flutes
- Faceted crystal spheres

- Wind chimes
- Many others

To order cure items, receive a price list, or obtain Grandmaster Lin Yun's Feng Shui teaching schedule, please contact:

Yun Lin Temple
2959 Russell Street
Berkeley, CA 97405
Tel: 510-841-2347
Web: www.yunlintemple.org
Email: info@yunlintemple.org

About the Author

DAVID DANIEL KENNEDY is a disciple of H.H. Grandmaster Lin Yun, and is the founder of the International Institute for Grandmaster Lin Yun Studies. Mr. Kennedy is a teacher, speaker, and professional consultant whose clients range from individuals to Fortune 500 companies. An expert at making Eastern concepts easily accessible, he has spent years showing students and the public how to make simple life changes that dramatically improve their wealth, reputation, relationships, and personal health.

His unique approach has delighted audiences at his speaking engagements and workshops throughout the United States and abroad, establishing him as one of the best-known writers and consultants on the subject. Mr. Kennedy is author of the bestselling *Feng Shui for Dummies*® and *Feng Shui Tips for a Better Life,* distributed worldwide in over ten languages.

For additional information on Feng Shui, consulting services, or Mr. Kennedy's unique and comprehensive training programs, contact:

International Institute for Grandmaster Lin Yun Studies
1563 Solano Avenue, Suite 127
Berkeley, CA 94707
Toll free: 888-470-2727
Web: www.daviddanielkennedy.com
Email: info@daviddanielkennedy.com

CD SESSIONS